ryan giggs

my story

ryan giggs

to my mum, Lynne,
and my grandparents,
Dennis and Margaret

my story

First published in Great Britain in 1994 by

Manchester United Football Club plc

Old Trafford

Manchester

M16 0RA

in association with

Virgin Publishing Ltd.

332 Ladbroke Grove

London

W10 5AH

A catalogue record for this book is available from the British Library.

ISBN 1 85227 459 X

Produced by **Zone Ltd.**

Designed by **offspring**

Studio photography: **Tim O'Sullivan**/Frank Spooner Pictures

Other photography: **John Peters, Action Images, Allsport, Sportsview**

Printed in Italy

contents

introduction

As I climbed the famous Wembley steps that soaking wet afternoon in May, it suddenly occurred to me how lucky I was. I was there, walking past the photographers snapping away, past the fans cheering, slapping my back and handing over silly hats and I couldn't believe what had happened...

In less than three years I had won a League Cup Winners' medal, two League Champions' awards and now here I was going up to collect an FA Cup Winners' medal, the oldest club trophy in the world. What's more, I was climbing the steps with Eric Cantona, the coolest bloke south of the North Pole, Mark Hughes, who had been my hero as long as I could remember, Paul Ince, owner of probably the loudest jacket seen next to a Championship trophy in football history, and Gary Pallister, who is very tall. And I was a member of the Manchester United side which had just completed the Double, only the fourth time it had been achieved by an English club this century. As I say, lucky or what?

It was a brilliant feeling. Before the game, the lads had been saying that nothing beats winning the FA Cup. Even winning the League for two years running wasn't as great a moment as when they won the Cup in 1990 - if only because we hadn't actually been playing either time we won the titles. I could see their point. I hadn't really appreciated how big the FA Cup was: the build-up, the interest, the noise on the day are all enormous, bigger than in any other game you play. Really, the League Cup is nothing in comparison. The Final begins a week beforehand. From the Sunday before the papers are full of comments and interviews; the television people are camped outside your hotel; and the highlight of the week is seeing your team-mates making idiots of themselves on *Top of The Pops*.

Once you get inside the stadium on the day, the noise, the colour and the excitement all really set the adrenalin boiling, really get you fired up. I hadn't played well on my last couple of appearances at Wembley. I'd been substituted in both the Coca Cola Cup Final and the Charity Shield, and I was determined to make my mark in the old stadium. In the first few minutes, the only mark I made was the indent left on the turf where I fell on it. A tackle by Chelsea's Erland Johnsen sent me into orbit. It certainly woke me up. It took us a while to settle down and Chelsea were on top in the first half. But in the opening minute of the second half I had a shot, then a few minutes later, I had a run down the wing and passed the ball inside to Denis Irwin. He went flying under a tackle and there was no question from anyone when the penalty was given. Up stepped Eric Cantona, the ice man. He wasn't worried about nerves. And that, as it usually is when Eric takes a penalty, was that. From then on, we enjoyed ourselves. Really enjoyed ourselves.

The final whistle. We had won 4-0 and secured the Double and the feeling was just brilliant! We jumped around, sprayed each other with water, put a silly wig on the Boss's head. Then when we followed Steve Bruce up the steps, it came to me. I was really lucky to be here. After all, if things had gone slightly differently, I might have been playing for Manchester City.

early days

It was probably the best birthday surprise I've ever had. I'd just turned fourteen and was sitting at home in Swinton, near Manchester, with my mum when there was a ring at the door. It was Alex Ferguson, manager of Manchester United...

Now I had reached fourteen, I could sign schoolboy forms with a professional club. He wanted to know if I was interested in signing them with Manchester United. If the manager of Manchester United comes round to your house, you tend to be a bit flattered. It's a rather nice feeling and not the kind of offer you turn down. I thought: *yes!* But my mum said she'd let him know.

My school photograph from Grosvenor Road school in Swinton, where I first started to play football properly.

In my gran's garden. Someone has taken the ball off me. They probably play for Arsenal now.

Even before I met the Boss I had my own technique for avoiding the media.

I started playing football properly when we moved up north when I was seven. Up till then I hadn't done much more than kick around in the garden with my grandad and my dad. Then my dad, Danny Wilson, who played stand-off half for Cardiff Rugby Club, signed as professional to play rugby league for Swinton. Shortly after we all moved up to live near the ground, which is in a suburb north of Manchester. I managed to get into my school team, Grosvenor Road Primary. A man called Denis Schofield saw me one day when we were playing and asked my mum if she would send me along to Dean's, a youth football club in Salford. She saw a good opportunity to get me out of the house, so I went along. In my first game, we lost 9-1.

To be honest I don't think I was an exceptional player at ten or eleven. I was quick and that was about it. I could always run fast. It was an asset I picked up from my dad who had a blistering turn of pace on the rugby field. My mum was very sporting too; she used to play baseball in Cardiff and netball. But Denis Schofield was a very good coach. At Dean's I learnt how to play football, how to read the game and know what to do. I realised it was about more than just running.

A handy jumper this. I could see this looking very fetching down the nightclubs now.

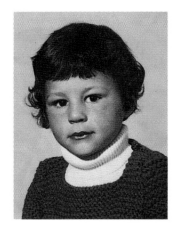

Another shot of the early fashion victim.

I also met up with a bunch of lads there who, because I never had to move away when I signed as a professional, are still my mates today. My mum says this is why I've not gone mad with all the fame. If I get big-headed, the lads can always take me down a peg or two, reminding me of how I was when I was a little kid. They all still play for a local pub team and I go and watch them in action as often as I can. I can never turn out to play for them, as I don't think the Boss would take too kindly to the news that I had injured myself playing in the Eccles League, Sunday Division. My mate Stuart wanted me to manage the team at one stage, but I don't think they need me. He scored pots of goals last season, so many he started calling himself the Onion Bag Engineer. No, I'm not sure, either.

When I was about eleven, a lot of us from Dean's were asked to a trial for Salford Schoolboys. I was always injured or on holiday or something - anyway, I missed it. So I got put in the Salford B team, while Stuart and the others were in the A side. On my debut I scored six goals. I didn't play for the B team again.

Salford Schoolboys were a good side. There were seven of us from Dean's, but the best player was a lad called Ben Thornley, who was a year younger than anyone else and used to play left wing. I was left midfield at the time. Ben made his debut for United last season, coming on as sub at West Ham. We were all gutted for him when he suffered a Gazza-style knee injury right at the end of the season play-

We quite often went to Jersey on holiday to the Battle of the Flowers. Check the shirt: the Six Million Dollar Man. I loved that shirt. $6 million wouldn't buy you a Wimbledon full back these days.

Me, my little brother Rhodri and Vinny Jones. Actually Carrie, my gran's dog.

An early bath for me and Rhodri

ing for the reserves. If he can fight back from that, he's some prospect.

I first played at Old Trafford for Salford. We got through to the final of the English School Cup, the first time the Salford lads had managed it for 48 years. We were playing St Helens and the first leg had been at Anfield. For the home game, about three thousand people turned up and sat in the main stand at Old Trafford. I was the captain that day, but usually Stuart was skipper. Before the game we made arrangements that we'd lift the cup together, a bit like Brucie and Robbo did with the Premiership trophy this year. But, inevitably, we lost. Even so I looked around the place, the dressing rooms, the facilities and I thought: yes, I'll have some of that. And fortunately I've been on the winning side when trophies have been picked up there since.

About this time I started playing rugby too. I'd always liked rugby and I used to follow Swinton when Dad was there, used to watch him play every Sunday. They were a good side then, on the up. They've slipped a bit now, though, and they sold their ground and play at Bury's football ground. These days I go and watch Wigan instead. I usually go along with Brian Kidd, who is always on the look-out for new training methods. He studies other sports

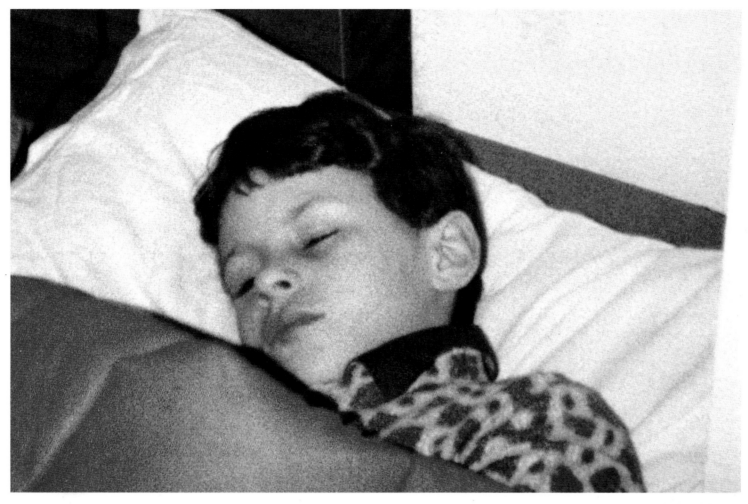

*A hard day's training can
take it out of a player*

incessantly to check out the way they operate and see if there's anything he can use for us. Me, I just like to see them beating the hell out of each other.

Anyway, I played for Salford Boys at rugby. We were a terrible side, always getting thrashed by St Helens, or Wigan 50-0,60-0,70-0. They all had these gorillas who gave us a right bashing. I got selected for the North of England side,

though, and at one time I was seriously thinking about concentrating on the game.

In those days I was playing for Salford at rugby, for two Dean's teams and for Salford Schoolboys at football, often four games in a weekend. There's a lot of debate about young lads playing too much too young and burning themselves out. I remember a bit later the Boss took me into his

In Jersey again, watching the flowers wearing a Paddington Bear shirt. Better not let Gary Pallister see it - he's always on the lookout for fashion tips.

Me and Rhodri on the sofa.
Watching A Question of Sport probably.

office once and said that he reckoned I'd played 85 match-es that season and it was too much for a young lad. But to be honest, I think it toughened me up, particularly the rugby. I was quite tall and skinny for my age, and happy just to run away from tackles. Rugby taught me how to get stuck in. Mind you, I don't think I would have made it if I had tried to follow my dad into the game. I haven't filled out enough in the upper body and I would have got hammered every week.

Denis Schofield was a scout for Manchester City, and when I was about twelve he suggested that I go down to City's Centre of Excellence for junior players. So another lad called Stuart and I used to go down there regularly every Thursday night. We'd work on skills, train. It was very good for me. Thanks, City!

But I was always a United fan. Swinton and Salford where I grew up is very much a red zone. I had been going to games at Old Trafford from the moment we moved up to Manchester. My dad took me to my first game there. It was against Sunderland and United won 1-0. But the thing I

remember most was that Mickey Thomas was playing - he's Welsh, you see - and I was always on the look-out for Welsh footballers. Then, when I got a bit older, all my mates from Dean's and I used to go to every home match and stand on the Stretford End. By then, my big United heroes were Bryan Robson and Mark Hughes.

Even so, I thought that if anyone was going to sign me as a professional, it would be City. These days, thanks to the Boss and Brian Kidd, United now sign the best young play-ers in the Manchester area. But when I was growing up, City had a great record at discovering local talent: Steve

Me with my grandparents who I used to call Nangy and Bampa.
I'm wearing a Wales away shirt given to me as a Christmas present. England shirts were not allowed in the house.

Redmond, Paul Lake and David White, who lived just down the road from me, all went to Maine Road. With Denis Schofield being a City scout, it just seemed that's where I'd play. But when I was thirteen I got asked to trials at United. What happened was that the mother of one of the other lads at Dean's was a mad United fan and she knew her newsagent was a scout for the club. She badgered him, hassled him, made his life a misery telling him to come and watch me. She said she'd never forgive him if I went to City, how she'd buy her papers from another shop.

In the end he came and I got invited for a trial. I played against another team of United trialists and got three in a 4-3 win. The other side gave me some gyp afterwards as I

Showing an early talent at babysitting. Knowing how to handle infants is a useful skill when we play at Elland Road.

My gran and me model the new Wales kit at my mum's wedding to Richard, my stepfather, in 1989.

Later that evening: an early sighting of the look I now give the Boss when he tells me I'm sub.

don't think I exactly enhanced their chances.

I really enjoyed myself and liked everything I saw, but I thought that was it because I didn't hear anything else and continued training with City. Then on my fourteenth birthday Alex Ferguson, the Boss, came round to the house. I was all up for it and wanted to sign there and then. But my mother, being the honourable woman she is, wanted to do the decent thing by City, because they'd been good to me. So she went to see Ken Barnes, their chief scout, to give them first refusal. She asked him if he was going to sign me and he said no, he wasn't. Not interested. So she got back in touch with Mr Ferguson, as she still calls him. And that, I'm pleased to say, was that.

heroes & villains

Because they were brilliant and they were Welsh, Mark Hughes and Ian Rush were my heroes when I was a lad. They still are, actually...

When I was an apprentice I used to really respect Gary Lineker. I used to play up front then and the coaches used to say to me, 'Watch Gary Lineker.' Because he was the best. I used to study the way he got into the box at the right

Sources of inspiration:
Mark Hughes
Ian Rush
Gary Lineker
Roberto Baggio

time, the way he judged his runs. He was brilliant at coming to the ball, checking and then getting behind defenders on their shoulders. The thing about him and Ian Rush is they can be rubbish all game, do nothing, then get one chance and score. Me, I miss far too many. The thing I used to admire about Rush was he seemed to always mis-hit the ball and it went in. If he had hit it too sweetly it would have missed completely, or the 'keeper would have been in the right place, so he would mis-hit it deliberately. He didn't care what it looked like as long as it went in.

These days I think the best player in the world is Roberto Baggio. He plays for Juventus and they've not had the best of times recently, but he's still miles ahead of anyone else in Italy. I've never seen him play in the flesh, just on the telly, but I could watch him play all week. He's a similar player to Eric, a good passer, a good goal-scorer who makes opportunities for others. And talking of Eric, I think he is coming up to be one of the best players in the world now.

I always enjoy playing against Chris Waddle too. He's a tremendous player, who seems to get better. The last few seasons he's been brilliant. Perhaps he's lost a touch of his pace but he's such a skilful player, a great passer of the ball, and he takes a wonderful corner. A model for wingers everywhere. He's hilarious to play against, doesn't stop taking the mickey. One of the many games last season when

Cool customers:
Eric Cantona
Chris Waddle
Gary Kelly
Earl Barrett

we played Sheffield Wednesday, he had the ball facing me, jinked a few times, dummied a few times and I ended up on the floor. I said to him: 'Hey steady down, it's us youngsters supposed to do that to you old timers.' He said: 'You steady down, then I'll steady down.' Then he suggested we make a deal; we'd both just walk around, have a nice stroll, enjoy the scenery.

It is not just goal-scorers who demand respect. There are several full-backs in the Premiership I have had great tussles with. Gary Kelly of Leeds played really well against me at Old Trafford this season, though I managed to get the better of him at Elland Road. He seems to be a player with a real future. I rate him. Generally, the older full-backs, peo-

ple like Earl Barrett at Aston Villa who are both quick and experienced, give you the least space and the most trouble.

You do get full-backs who try to intimidate you, saying how hard they are and how many lumps they're going to kick out of you. But I'm used to that. When I was younger I always played with boys older than me. So I was used to people trying to bully me out of it. When players start threatening you, take it as a compliment. It shows they are wary about what you can do to them with the ball. Besides, there are few more pleasurable experiences on a football field than taking the mick out of defenders who have a go at you. I love that feeling of knocking the ball past a defend-

er and going. Just as he thinks he'll get a tackle in, you touch it a little bit more and you're away.

Toward the end of last season, teams started putting two players on me, the midfield player dropping back to help the full-back. They would double up to try and stop me and Andrei or Sharpey, thinking that was a way to stifle United. They don't stop you playing as such, but they cut off the supply to you, the ball just comes over less frequently. We've worked on ways to combat this in training, but I'm not going to say what they are. Wait and see.

the Boss

There's more to Alex Ferguson than just keeping me from the press. Without him, I wouldn't be where I am today. From the moment he came to the house that day when I was fourteen he has helped me develop...

He didn't just protect me from outside influences which might have deflected me from concentrating on my football at a time when I needed to concentrate on that alone, he also protected me physically. As I said, when I was a schoolboy he

called me into his office and said that he had worked out I had played eighty-five games that season and it was too much. I couldn't tell what he was on about at the time, because I felt as if I could play double that. But he had had an experience with a young player at Aberdeen who was brilliant as a kid and he just burnt him out, asked too much of him too soon.

So when I broke into the first team, he was always careful to rest me, dropping me to sub or off the team completely when he thought I was getting a bit jaded. You see, if you're not feeling well, or an injury is nagging at you, it's up to you to say so. But I never would because I always

want to play. There have been times when the gaffer's said, 'I'm not going to play you this week,' and I was fed up because I thought I was all right. There were other times, though, when he told me not to play which were absolutely right. I wasn't up to it and he seems to be able to see straight through me and read that. He's always honest about it. He'll have a quiet word with you in advance to say he's going to drop you and why. During the week he'll pull you into his office and say: 'Listen, I'm playing Sharpey' or 'You need a break.'

Another thing is that tactically he's unbelievable. He can spot things going wrong so fast, plug gaps, see openings.

If I'm getting no change out of a full back, he'll swap me over with Andrei or Sharpey, or bring me inside. He communicates what's wrong to the players really well. Too well sometimes. If I'm doing something wrong he'll come down to the touch-line and scream instructions to me. Sometimes he'll still be screaming at me when the ball comes to me; I turn round to listen to what he's shouting, let the ball go and hear him yell, 'Watch the game.'

At half-time in the FA Cup final, the Boss said to me, 'You can win the game for us.' What he meant was not that he expected some amazing bit of skill from me but that a simple alteration in the position I was playing could make all the difference. In the first half, Chelsea's midfield was running it and Andrei and me were too far out on the wings, giving them too much space inside. So he moved us in. They didn't change tack and they didn't get a kick in the second half. He's also very good at spotting your individual weakness. Something I've got to work on is my vision of what's going on around me. A lot of people, my mum included, thought that a goal I scored against QPR last season was the best I've scored. I got the ball on the halfway line and beat about four men before banging it past the keeper. But at the time, I didn't realise how many people I'd beaten. I just put my head down and went for goal and I honestly thought I'd had a free run at it. It wasn't until I got home and saw it on the telly that I thought: hold on, where did he come from?

Well, that would never happen with Eric Cantona, who seems to know exactly where everyone is, opponents and colleagues both, as soon as he gets the ball. When I first got into the team it was just head down and take people on, which the crowd like when it comes off but is pretty pointless when it doesn't. The Boss had a word with me and said: 'You don't have to beat a player every time, sometimes give a simple pass and that will keep the defender guessing, he won't be certain what you're trying to do.' It's something you learn with experience, knowing when to take someone on and when to pass it. And the Boss is very good at making sure you learn quickly. He's a brilliant teacher.

When you join United they teach you from the start how to play football. If you think about it, the youth team coaches have got to be the best coaches in the club. The first team coach has world class players to work with, but the youth team coach is dealing with people who have just come into the game. He has to give them the knowledge to enable them to go on into the first team. The youth coaches, Eric Harrison, and when I was first there, Nobby Stiles, are just brilliant.

Whether a manager has to have been a great player to be a great manager I'm not sure. The Boss wasn't, as he's always telling us. Obviously, he's got to be a decent player, got to know what's going on; but managing is more about motivation. The Boss is fantastic at that. He drives us on and stops us ever becoming complacent. He's always asking us if we feel hungry enough for the challenge ahead, and if we don't there are five people he knows who do.

He proved that over the summer, snapping up David May from Blackburn. He's a class act, May, very comfortable on the ball, a defender who will fit in well with our style of play. Just like the fans, we players speculate on who could be joining us, but of all the names bandied around, May's wasn't one of them, not because we didn't rate him, but because he was at Blackburn. We thought he was out of bounds. But that kind of thing doesn't stop the Boss. He's brilliant in the transfer market and to nick the best defender from our closest rivals was a stroke. It could prove as sharp as pinching Eric from Leeds.

Mind you, for all his preparation, the Boss is madly superstitious. If we lose a game away from home he won't stay at the same hotel the next time we play. If we win, he makes sure we go through exactly the same routine next time in our preparations. That kind of approach is catching; if I play well I try to do the same things before the next game too, I eat the same thing, get ready in the same way. But it never seems to work!

Wales

Apparently, Terry Venables said to the Boss that he couldn't believe that I was allowed to slip through the English net and play for Wales. It's flattering, but there was never any question of playing for England...

To be fair to the Boss, even though he's not exactly one to go out of his way to help the English cause, he did once take me into his office and say I'd stand a better chance of playing in the World Cup if I made myself available for selection by England. But if I was going to be lucky enough to play for a country, it had to be Wales.

I was born in Wales, so were my mum and dad and my grandparents. I know I captained England Schoolboys and talk with a Manchester accent, but I am Welsh. Manchester is the town I live and work in: it happens to be in England. Wales is my country.

Besides, I don't think Mum would have forgiven me if I'd turned out for England. For as long as I can remember she would scream for Wales in the Five Nations rugby, sitting on the sofa in front of the telly with tears rolling down her cheeks when the Welsh national anthem came on. No, she wouldn't have forgiven me, she'd have lynched me.

Now, I'm incredibly proud when I put on that Welsh shirt. I don't sing the anthem before matches quite as well as my mum but I know the words, despite what my mates reckon. We were taught them at school in Wales, and my grandad was forever drumming the anthem into me.

I made my debut against Germany in Nuremberg in 1991. I came on as sub, the youngest ever cap for Wales. Lothar Matthaus, Thomas Doll, Effenberg and Klinsmann were all playing for Germany. They were class. I didn't get a kick.

Funnily enough, I found it surprisingly easy to settle into the Welsh set-up. Ian Rush and Mark Hughes had been my heroes for as long as I could remember, but then I found out that they, and the other older lads like Neville Southall, were also unbelievably welcoming. Kevin Ratcliffe said an amazing thing to the press when I made my debut: that he could now tell his grandchildren that he had played with Ryan Giggs. That doesn't half relax you.

Another good thing about playing for Wales is there's no pressure on us whatsoever. There's none of the media slag-offs the England lads have to put up with. And it's great for me because the team hotel in Cardiff is about ten minutes from where my grandparents live so I've got loads of friends and relatives around. It feels like home.

There may be none of the hype there is with the England team, but that doesn't mean the crowd isn't passionately behind you. Since I've been in the Welsh team, they've played at Cardiff Arms Park. The atmosphere is just brilliant. The lads who have been in for some time, who played at Wrexham and Ninian Park, say it's worth a goal compared to those days. When I scored on my full debut, against

Belgium, you could have heard the noise at Wembley.

It's not all joy playing for your country, though. I was very disappointed not to qualify for the World Cup. Realistically, it was the best chance we had for years to get there. We had a well-balanced side with young players like Gary Speed and me, and the old heads like Saunders, Hughes, Rush and Southall. I reckon we'd have stood a good chance of doing well in America. I'm not the only one from United who didn't go: France blew it even worse than we did (Eric was well fed up with that), Denmark didn't get there, we know what happened to England and even Andrei, whose mob qualified, fell out with his manager and didn't make it. So in a squad full of internationals, only Roy and Denis had the experience of playing there. And, boy, did they let us know they were the only ones going.

We in the Wales team have only ourselves to blame for not going to America, however. We had such a bad start, losing 5-1 away to Romania. I was on the subs' bench and came on for the last twenty minutes of that game. It was the worst twenty minutes I've ever had on a football pitch. They were just brilliant and Hagi, their schemer, was unbelievable.

By the time we beat Belgium at home we had recovered from that and were on a roll. In the end what we had to do was beat Romania in the return match in Cardiff to qualify. We went into the game thinking we had to win by two clear

goals, but as it turned out just one would have done it. When things are going well for them, the Romanians are untouchable. But the moment things go wrong, their heads go down. It was amazing in that game; they took an early lead, which we got back to 1-1 and as soon as we equalised and started to get on top, Hagi went on to the wing and sulked. You could see it, he just didn't want the ball. I've never seen anything like it, a player of his genius just disappearing when qualifying for the World Cup hinged on the result. I thought we would do it then, especially

when we got a penalty, but Paul Boden missed. After the penalty I had half a chance. But I missed. Then as we piled forward, they got a breakaway and that was it.

In the dressing room afterwards there was nothing to say. It was complete silence, the lowest I've ever felt. And I was luckier than some. There were lads in there who had given everything for years to Wales and they knew their chance had gone. Terry Yorath was brilliant that night. He said to us all: 'Listen, it was the best you could do. We came so close.'

I really rate Terry Yorath as a manager. It was hard for him at first - he wasn't sure whether to play four at the back or a sweeper - but once he got everything sorted out we started playing really well. He had a good laugh with the lads, treated us like adults. Peter Shreeves took the training and he was brilliant. You can't compare Terry's approach to the Boss's because it is a completely different thing managing a club from a country, but I rate him very highly.

Then after all his work, all his effort, he was allowed to go. Immediately after the World Cup campaign, when he had done so much, he was kicked out. It seems to me that something should have been done to allow him to stay as manager, especially as his son had died less than a year before he was released. We couldn't believe it. Everyone wanted him to stay, the players, the fans, Terry himself.

I suppose we shouldn't have been surprised. Frankly, the Welsh operation at that time was a mess. After Yorath came John Toshack. I was injured for a game and missed the whole of his reign, which, according to the lads, was characterised by some well bizarre ideas. Now the secretary of the Welsh FA has resigned, things have settled down a bit. Perhaps we'll be able to get back to playing football under Mike Smith.

It won't be easy. For the 1996 European Championship we've got a really difficult draw again: Germany, Albania, Bulgaria. It's going to be hard to qualify, but I'm desperate to go to a major championship with Wales. Even if it is in England.

a united player

I couldn't believe how high the standard was at United. I'd done a lot of training at City, and the other schoolboys there weren't that brilliant. At United, I was knocked out.

The system worked out was that I would play for the B team or the A team at the weekend and in the school holidays I would go to United and train with them for a week. The first Christmas holidays after I signed, when I came down to the Cliff, I just couldn't believe how good everyone was. There was a lad called Raphael Burke there and he was the best schoolboy in England at the time. Absolutely

brilliant. He hasn't made it now, but at fourteen he was unstoppable. Alan Thompson who plays for Bolton now was there too. And Nick Barmby. He wanted to sign for United, and at one point it looked as though he was going to. But in the end he was persuaded to sign for Tottenham instead. With players like that in the side, when we played other teams, we were so good.

I was lucky then because I could play in the A team. These days there are so many talented young players at Old Trafford, a schoolboy rarely gets a game even in the B team. They've just started an under-16s side to compensate.

When I was fifteen, I was also captain of the England Schoolboys team. We were a good side, with Nick Barmby and Darren Caskey, who also plays for Spurs now. In my nine matches as captain, we won seven, including turning over Germany, Holland, France and Belgium.

As you can imagine, at this time I didn't exactly concentrate on my schoolwork. Football was everything and I took no interest in anything other than sport at school. Perhaps that was a mistake. Some of the teachers didn't mind: the PE teachers were very encouraging, really helped me, and the headmaster was good, because he was a keen footballer too. My school work was particularly bad when I was in the fourth year. I was playing for England Schoolboys and United were always asking me down for extra training so I took a lot of time off, but the school was always very accommodating, understanding if my homework was non-

existent. Only a couple of the teachers used to grumble: my English teacher and my history teacher. They were women and they weren't too happy about my absences. To be honest, I don't blame them.

I used to travel with the United youth team a lot when I was still a schoolboy. Once when we were in Italy in a tournament, the referee had to check us off against a list of passports, like a school register. I think it was to make sure we were all the right age to qualify for the competition - it was about the time the Mexicans were slipping thirty-year-olds into their under-21s. When he read out the passports, the name on mine was Giggs. All my teachers, the people

at Dean's, everyone at United knew me as Ryan Wilson then and everyone looked round, wondering who this Giggs character was. I said it was me. The reason it was Giggs was because it was my mum's maiden name and that was the name on my birth certificate, so it was the name on the passport. That was the first time the name came out.

When I left school I made a decision to call myself Giggs. My mum and dad had split up by then, and my mum remarried. My mum's side of the family had been brilliant in my upbringing and I suppose I wanted the world to know I was my mother's son. I belong to her family. I still see an awful lot of my two aunties, uncles and my grandparents. They have always seemed to take most pleasure in life from taking the mickey out of me: my aunt is still at it, asking me when I'm going to turn into a real man, like Eric Cantona.

As soon as I left school, at sixteen, I signed as an appren-

tice for United, a YTS trainee. I got £29.50 a week plus £10 expenses. And it went up a fiver when I was seventeen. From then on you train full-time, and I mean full-time, morning and afternoon. I think I was lucky because I came from Manchester. George Best told me he was very unhappy when he arrived here from Belfast at the age of seventeen; in fact he ran back homesick after he'd been here less than a week. I can see how that happened, living in digs in a strange city. But I was living at home with my mum and her cooking, I could see my mates at the weekends and I knew a lot of the older apprentices from playing with them in the A team every Saturday. I found everyone very welcoming, including the senior players. I remember the first senior player I spoke to was Viv Anderson, who is now at Middlesbrough, assistant manager to Bryan Robson. I played in a practice game against the first team, and I was

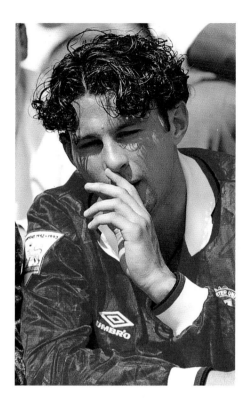  

up against him, so he chatted to me, telling me to slow down.

For most of the 1990/91 season, my second at the club, I played for the A team. I'd been enjoying it, popping in the odd goal, but I thought I still had a long way to go. One week in March, I'd been training with the reserves or the youth team as usual. Then on the Friday Brian Kidd came into the apprentice dressing room and said: 'You're training with us today.' Off I went with the big boys: Robson, Hughes, the players I had watched from the terraces. After the training session he simply said: 'Report to Old Trafford at midday tomorrow'. A couple of the older players started winding me up, saying: 'You're playing, son.' So the next day I got there as instructed, a squadron of butterflies flapping in my stomach. There were about sixteen players in the squad, and I honestly thought I was there to make up

numbers, there for the experience. The Boss doesn't usually announce his team until an hour before a game. I was astonished to be named as sub.

People often ask me what it was like making my debut in front of 44,000 people at Old Trafford. Well, it was this: brilliant. I'd played there for the reserves and the youth team, so perhaps I wasn't as daunted by the place as someone signed from a lesser club might be, but I was still well nervous. Walking out of the tunnel, seeing all those faces merging into one, hearing the noise, it's an experience you'd be pushed to describe if you were Clive James. I was sitting on the bench, nervous, very nervous. But once we went 2-0 up and there was no chance of us losing, I was desperate to go on. And when I did, I was quite relaxed. There were a lot of injuries at the time and I played up front alongside Lee Sharpe and Danny Wallace. Looking back on the video of that game, what I think now is: what was that haircut?

I was much more nervous when I made my full debut against City a couple of weeks later. I enjoyed it even better, though: I scored. Well, I didn't. It was a goal-mouth scramble. It hit me, then hit someone else, then hit Colin Hendry and went in. It was an own goal, but the defender didn't want to take responsibility. So, as it was my debut, the boss told the press I'd got it. I was seventeen and I wasn't going to argue with that. It was in the papers the next day as mine, and no matter how much Incey takes the mickey out of me about it, it remains mine.

During that close season I thought, 'I've got no chance here.' Lee Sharpe had won the PFA Young Player of the Year award, had been brilliant in the run to the European Cup Winners' Cup and, what's more, he was left wing, my position. I felt I was in for a long, long wait. When the new season started, I thought I should just aim for the reserves and keep plugging at it, try and play well, just keep in everyone's mind. Then, quite early on, Sharpey got injured. I was in the squad, against Notts County, then on the Wednesday I was sub against Aston Villa; after that I was in the team. When I got into the first team I started getting letters from people asking me if I was the Ryan Wilson who played for England Schoolboys.

People thought it was a bit of an overnight thing: seventeen-year-old makes his debut in the first team. Anyone who thinks that obviously doesn't know about football. There was a long evening of hard work: six, seven years of living, breathing, eating and sleeping football before it happened. And once it had happened, I wasn't about to let it go.

routine

Some people seem to think being a footballer involves nothing more strenuous than waking up on a Saturday morning and playing in the afternoon. It's never like that...

And not just because we play most of our matches on a Sunday these days because of television.

All of us train hard, even Incey who, given the choice, would rather stay in bed. I enjoy training, I feel frustrated if I haven't come away from a session having learned some-

thing or improved on an aspect of my game. Brian Kidd is brilliant at leading the training. He studies all sorts of methods and always has new ideas. Half way through last season, he went to Italy, to Milan and Parma to study their methods and came back saying all they do is shooting practice. So in the afternoons, it became a bit of a habit for a group of us to stay on and do some shooting practice. It was usually Eric, Incey, Andrei, Roy and me trying to bury it past Peter or Les. Kiddo often stops off too. I found it really helped.

Towards the end of the season, though, when we're playing Sunday, Monday, Wednesday - and soon midnight on Thursday - you just can't do it. We have to rest, recuperate, get our energy back. Training becomes no more than a quick jog, some five-a-side and then lying on the treatment table. You really can't work on your technique, which everyone needs to do no matter what level they are at. When you see Eric Cantona brushing up his skills, you know that no one can be satisfied with their standard. We players keep saying we play too much football, and that being too tired to train properly is not good for the game. But nobody seems to listen. In Italy, the season starts later and is all over nearly a month before ours, and we're expected to cope on the same terms as them in the European Cup. When Eric was out with his suspension, you could tell in training the difference between him and us. With his enforced rest, he was really fresh and alert, dying to get back. And he showed how much he had benefited from the break when he scored two on his first game back against Manchester City.

The rule at the club is that you can't go out for three nights before a game. That restriction can be a pain, particularly since we play so many games on a Sunday and my mates are all out on Friday and Saturday night. Actually, they're pretty good to me. They don't tempt me out. In fact a few of them will come round and keep me company in front of the video. I watch a lot of football videos: Kiddo gives me stacks of them to study, to watch how others play. Homework if you like.

On a match day we are expected to report three hours before kick-off. If it's a Saturday, we all have a meal in the grill room at Old Trafford and then head to the players' lounge, where the papers are laid out and where you can watch Football Focus. Some of the lads have a bet and enjoy the racing on TV but, to be honest, I find the hanging around gets tedious. I can't wait to get on with it. About an hour before kick-off, the Boss calls us in for a team talk. This takes about twenty minutes and he runs through the opposition, their strengths and weaknesses, and any special roles he might have for us. Actually he usually says: 'Just go out and play your game.' When I made my debut he just said: 'Ryan, you're on the left.' Magic words. Eric couldn't have written a better poem than that. About thirty minutes before kick-off, we start to go through our warm-ups. Each player has got his own warm-up routine, there's a gym in the changing rooms where you mess around with the ball, do some stretches. Then about twenty minutes to kick off we go out on the pitch, do some stretches, have a kickabout. Eric, of course, has the flashest warm-up, stretching and toning up muscles the rest of us didn't even know we had.

Things have changed a lot in this regard since the old days. Bestie told me that, in his time, the team would meet up at a golf course in Bramhall, have a meal and a game of snooker, then go to the club about 45 minutes before kick-off. He'd then disappear and have a cup of tea with his mates in the players' lounge. He would be there until about five minutes before kick-off, then someone would come and find him and he'd go out on to the pitch, not warm up or anything. It's much more regimented with us, much more like a military campaign. Though it didn't seem to do him any harm did it?

One thing we would certainly not do is eat what they did just before a game back then. Best was a little ahead of his time, because he used to have bananas and Corn Flakes. But most of the team had steak, the worst thing to have. It's very slow to digest, steak, and sits in your stomach like a lead weight. These days we're made very much more aware of our diets and how they can affect our play. Halfway through the season, Trevor the club dietitian introduced a way of measuring body fat. I turned out to have the lowest body fat in the club, along with Eric of course: 8 per cent of body weight. The club reckon you've got to be below 15 per cent, and some of the older, bigger players find that a problem. Particularly Pally, who lives off a diet of junk: Mars bars, crisps, cans of Coke. Trevor and Kiddo really have a go at him to eat properly to get the body fat down. You have to feel sorry for Pally because Incey, who is more than partial to a Big Mac, can get away with it without apparently putting on any weight. We are supposed to eat pasta, grilled chicken, fish, which is fortunate for me because I like that sort of food. The Boss organised for Sharpey and me to go to cookery lessons, so that, as single lads, we could learn how to cook properly. We enjoyed that: spent most of the time eating the stuff the demonstrator had cooked up for us. We are all issued with diet sheets;

I gave mine to my mum. It even says what biscuits you should eat: Jaffa cakes, Garibaldis and fig rolls, which have very little fat in them. So farewell chocolate Swiss roll fingers. A steak, incidentally, would be fine after a game, to replace some of the lost carbohydrates and so on, but you have to have light, easily digestible stuff beforehand.

If you are carrying a slight knock, you are taken for a late fitness test at the Cliff earlier in the morning. You usually know how you feel, and whether you're up for it, but our physiotherapist generally has something to say. This season I seem to have had more injuries than before, little knocks really, which I've played through. The worst injury of my career was in the derby against Manchester City, the first time Eric Cantona played as it happens. I had the ball on the wing, cut inside and shot. Steve McMahon came across to block me, put his foot up to stop the ball and, with my follow-through, I kicked the studs on the bottom of his boot. As you can imagine, Steve McMahon's studs are pretty hard. I made contact with the top of my foot, where there's very little protection and I think I pulled a ligament. Ask any footballer, and they'll say that for this to be your worst injury, you've been incredibly lucky. And I have. Touch wood. I have found I can usually duck out of a dodgy tackle; if you're quick enough you can jump out of the way in time. If someone's going to do you, you can feel it, sense it coming and take evasive action. It's always happened that opponents will try and clip you. If you play for Manchester

United, people want to take you down a peg or two. When I played for the A team it was particularly the case, especially in home matches which are played at the Cliff. You get quite a big crowd for an A team fixture, so the opposition wants to make an impression on you. On your ankles mainly. I only have to look around the Cliff to see how lucky I am. David Johnson and Ben Thornley, two of our best young players, have both had cruciate ligament damage

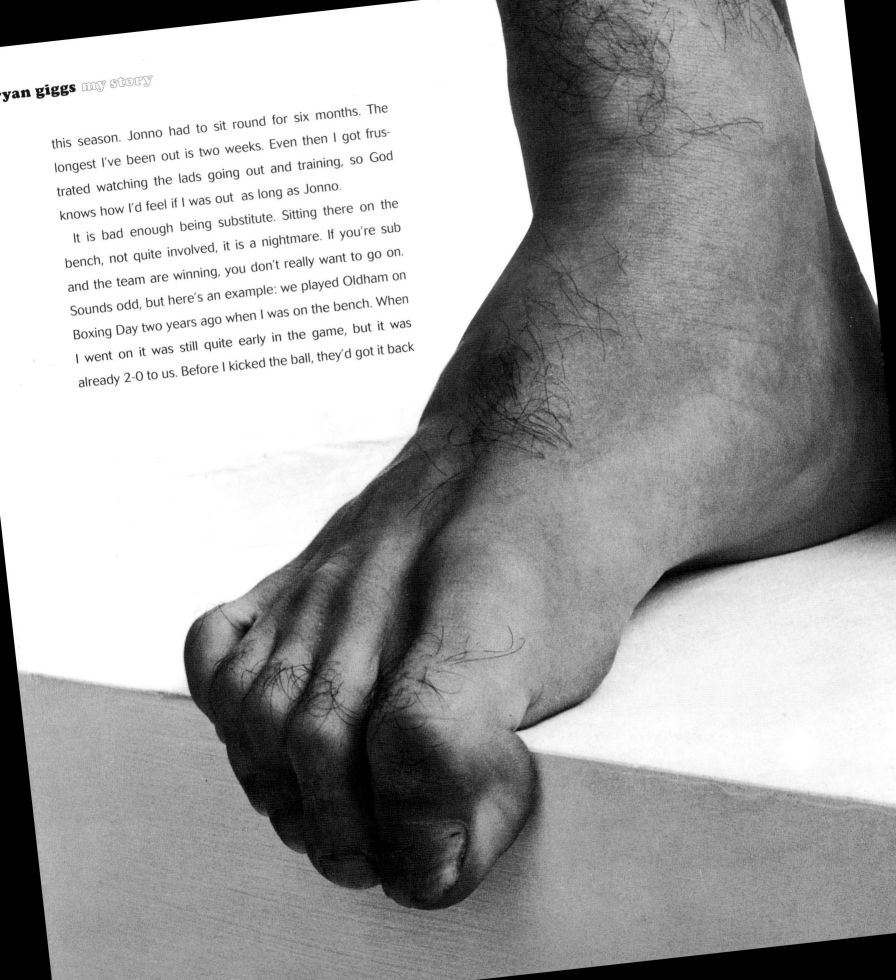

this season. Jonno had to sit round for six months. The longest I've been out is two weeks. Even then I got frustrated watching the lads going out and training, so God knows how I'd feel if I was out as long as Jonno.

It is bad enough being substitute. Sitting there on the bench, not quite involved, it is a nightmare. If you're sub and the team are winning, you don't really want to go on. Sounds odd, but here's an example: we played Oldham on Boxing Day two years ago when I was on the bench. When I went on it was still quite early in the game, but it was already 2-0 to us. Before I kicked the ball, they'd got it back to 2-2. I was thinking: 'They're all going to blame me. It will be my fault, there was only one difference between the team which was winning 2-0 and the one which was suddenly drawing 2-2. Me.' Luckily we went on to win 6-3. It is nice to come on and get the winner if you're losing, or make the killer pass, to play the role of super-sub. But the other way round, and you come on and lose: well, it's always the forward's fault.

So that's the usual routine. And given the amount of travel involved to away matches, you can see, there's not a lot of time for appearances on *Celebrity Squares*.

goals

Gazza said recently that scoring a goal was better than an orgasm. Lee Chapman said it wasn't as good. Me, I think I'll go with Pelé on this debate. He's a pretty switched-on geezer and he thought it was about the same. So it's pretty good fun scoring at Old Trafford. A goal, that is. That moment's intense pleasure is what it's all about.

57

The longest I've gone without scoring a goal is about seven games. As a winger, cutting in, sometimes you only get one chance. And then you kick yourself when you blow it. As I've said, I'm a terrible loser. Although I'd rather have a bad game which the team wins than play a blinder in a game we lose, if I miss a chance I still go into a right sulk and blame myself. So I've been working on improving my goal rate to reduce the number of times I feel that bad. Kiddo has given me videos to study the methods of great goalscorers, and last season I've popped in more than ever before, seventeen. It wasn't enough to win my bet with

Incey, though: I'd said I'd get twice what he scored and he got nine. I've scored more of the bread-and-butter goals too: like the one against Ipswich, a short-ranger against Norwich, one against Everton where I scored with a header, and they give me just as much pleasure as the dribbles and the spectacular ones, because they're goals which last year I wasn't scoring, the ones where you get into goal-scoring positions and pop the thing away.

When you score, you celebrate. Or not.

This season the celebrations have been getting dafter. I suppose that dance Incey and I did last year set a bit of a

fashion that has now got well out of hand. We planned it in training and said if we both scored in a game, then we'd do it. It was against Blackburn, the last game of the 1993 season, that we unveiled it. You can only do it when you're on your way to a victory, otherwise you look a bit foolish, standing there, intertwining legs and fingers. But last season, everyone was at it. Defenders who never score were doing little routines, people were doing somersaults, belly flops into the corner. There's a team in Brazil who all line up and then fall over in turn like a bunch of dominoes. It must take them hours on the training pitch working that one out. I can just imagine what the Boss would say if we tried to do something like that.

As for Sharpey, he did a number at Arsenal where he pretended to be Elvis: ran to the corner post, turned the collar of his shirt up, swivelled his hips and used the flag as a microphone. Elvis? He looked more like Val Doonican.

I reckon the coolest celebrations are the simple ones: Alan Shearer, both arms up; Andy Cole, one arm raised, finger pointing. Or Ian Wright: going completely mad, running two hundred yards then standing still doing something strange with his fingers. You've got to have respect for Ian Wright.

I decided that if I scored I'd try to do a celebration that wasn't a celebration. I tried not even to smile. I managed to perfect it at Leeds, just standing there in the box, not moving a muscle. But at Ipswich, the goal meant so much to us, I was really made up and I couldn't control myself: I just went mad. I think that's the way to do it, whatever comes naturally at the moment you score. So I think if I'd got that goal Hughesie scored to equalise against Oldham in the last seconds of the FA semi, I'd have run round Wembley twice, taken my shirt off, thrown it into the crowd, then dived in after it.

winning

When I joined the team, Manchester United were starting to win again. After a difficult period, Alex Ferguson was starting to get results. The team had won the FA Cup in 1990 and the Cup Winners' Cup in 1991, but the thing everyone craved was the League Championship...

That year it had become the FA Premier League and soon it was to be called the Premiership, but whatever its name, what counted among United followers was the Title. You couldn't escape knowing that it was twenty-five years since United had last won it in 1967, the days of Best, Law and Charlton. Everywhere you went people were reminding you of it, the media was full of it, fans would come to you in the street and say they hoped the wait was over. People said, 'Come on, make sure this is the one.' The expectation was there, on your shoulders, all the time.

In April 1992, we won the Rumbelows' League Cup at Wembley, my first senior trophy, and I passed to Brian McClair to score the winner. It was brilliant, but it wasn't the big one. That Easter we had a terrible fixture backlog and

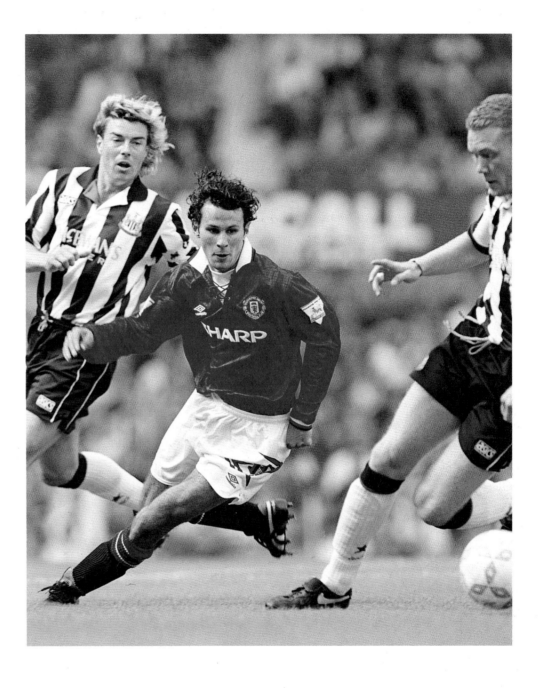

we blew it. We lost at home to Notts Forest, but the game that really did it for us was against West Ham when we lost 1-0. That was the day we knew we'd blown it. They had been rubbish all season, and suddenly they were brilliant against us. In the dressing room afterwards, we knew it had gone.

It became mathematically certain when we lost against Liverpool, of all people. We played at three o'clock and Leeds had played at Sheffield United at twelve. It was a farce: they won it with this ridiculous goal, a right joke soft one. So that was it, we went out against Liverpool knowing it was going to be twenty-six years at least before the big one came again. And the Liverpool fans really enjoyed us going down then. They loved it, loved the fact that even

though their team weren't what they were, at least we weren't going to win it. We lost, and the title was on its way to Leeds, a team who had been revitalised by a certain Frenchman.

It really hurt, blowing it in 1992. I'm a terrible loser. I hate losing at anything, no matter how trivial. Ask Incey what I'm like when he beats me at golf. Awful. And I should have plenty of practice, because he beats me every time. If I have a bad game for United, it's the worst. I go into the dressing room and I'm always last to get in the shower. I just sit there for half an hour, going over in my mind where it went wrong, where I could have made more of a contribution, working out how I missed that sitter. After that game against Liverpool I was very down. And it wasn't as bad for me as it was for the older players, Robbo and Brucie, who thought their chance had passed them by. It was my first season, after all. I can't imagine how bad it was for them. When I came out of the ground at Anfield, as I was walking towards the team coach, some Liverpool supporters asked for my autograph. I signed it for them and they tore the pieces of paper up in my face. I got back home and said to my mum that I had to get away. So I went for a couple of days down to Cardiff to my grandparents and tried to put the whole thing into perspective. What that kind of experience does is motivate you. It hurts so much, it makes you want to make sure it never happens again.

The next season it didn't. At first I thought we were never going to get anywhere. It was now twenty-six years since we last won the title and we were bottom of the table for the first couple of weeks, but then we pulled ourselves together and moved up. And we signed Eric Cantona from Leeds. That was the missing piece of the jigsaw. Eric is such an incredible character; his presence alone was enough to lift us, but he was a brilliant player too, the best in Britain, and pretty close to being the best in the world. With Eric on board we believed in ourselves completely. We were just determined it wasn't going to go the same way it had the previous year. The turning point was the game against Sheffield Wednesday at Old Trafford on Easter Saturday. The previous year, Easter had finished us off, but that year, just when it looked as if our chance had gone again, Brucie stepped up and scored the equaliser. Then, in so much injury time it was almost the next season by the time he did it, he scored the winner too. After that we knew it was our year. When it actually happened, we weren't playing. Aston Villa, our only challengers, were playing Oldham on the Monday and they had to win to keep their challenge going. It went out live on television and the Boss had banned us from watching the game. But I went round to a mate's house and though I couldn't bear to watch the first half, I

sneaked a look at the second. When Oldham won, we went mad, we all went out celebrating, people were coming up to me, congratulating me, all over the town. I ended up that night at Brucie's house, where all the players and their wives had gathered.

The next day we played Blackburn at home. The atmosphere was incredible, you could feel the twenty-six years' weight lifting off 40,000 shoulders. It had not been the stan-

dard preparation for a game the night before, and Blackburn were pretty determined to ruin the party. They went into an early lead, so I was pretty pleased to score the equaliser from a free kick. We went on to win, went up and picked up our medals and the trophies. After the game we partied some more. I thought that was as good as it could get.

Winning, we found, was addictive. We weren't satisfied. We just wanted more and more of it.

celebrity

I signed my first autograph when I was on tour with England Schoolboys. I was at a hotel with the team and this girl who worked in the kitchen was hanging out of the window. We were on our way out to the team coach and, as we walked past, she shouted to me to sign my autograph. The thing was my name was Ryan Wilson then, so she probably doesn't realise now whose signature she's got...

Once I broke into the first team at United, I started signing a few more. When you join the club it is made clear to you that you are representing Manchester United and you should behave accordingly. The Boss is also very clear that the people who want autographs are the people who give us our livelihood and that we owe them our time and our good manners. And that's absolutely right. We all try to sign as many as we can. That said, things can get out of hand. During school holidays, the Cliff, our training ground, gets overrun with people; thousands upon thousands turn up. My mum dropped me off there recently and a coach had just pulled up, and an entire party of sightseers was getting off. I said to Mum, 'Put your foot down and get me in quick.' On days like that there are so many people, I can't physically sign anything: I've got ten pieces of paper shoved in front of my nose, someone's pulling my arm, someone's grabbing my leg, someone else has trodden on my toe. I get more little knocks in the Cliff car park than I've ever got off Vinny Jones.

It's amazing, the interest there is in United. The youth team lads claim that after training they can tell who's gone into the car park from the changing room without even looking. If there's a lot of older blokes shouting, it's Eric. If it's girls screaming, it's Sharpey. And if there's no noise at all, it's Pally. Once in a really bad crush, Sharpey ran over a girl's foot with the wheel of his car. He was really worried, but she was pleased. Dead proud she was. Asked him if he could do it for her friend. I love the letters I get sent, too. At Valentine's Day I got sack-loads of stuff and it was just great. When I was in hospital having my tonsils out, I got sent fruit and all sorts. Someone sent me a bunch of balloons. They looked a bit like my tonsils, actually. All red and

swollen. People send amazing things, they make things for me, they send things to me, knit scarves, hats, jumpers, ties. They read I like soul music in a magazine, so they make up a tape of music specially, or send me a CD, which is incredibly kind. Girls have started sending me other things too, which my grandad, who handles all my mail, delights in telling me about. Fortunately not a lot shocks him. Even so, it's nothing compared to what George Best got in his heyday. When I met him, we worked out he got about five times as much mail.

It's a strange thing trying to come to terms with all this attention. One thing I still can't work out is when complete strangers let on to me in the street as if they know me: 'Hi Ryan how you doing?' they say. And I always start thinking: 'Do I know this person? Am I being rude not remembering them?'

To be a teenager and thrust into that is weird. Luckily for me I have grown up within the club, and I have been allowed to grow at my own pace without having to deal with all the pressures that have affected other players in the past, particularly from the media. And that's down to the Boss. He is brilliant at protecting the young players at United. It was the same for me and Sharpey; he didn't let the press or any of the commercial agents near either of us. For some reason everyone thought I was a special case and needed to be protected from the outside world to stop me becoming another George Best. But I wasn't a special case. None of the young players are allowed to talk to the press at Old Trafford and I think that's a brilliant thing. You're only eighteen or nineteen; you're not a pop star who wants to be in the limelight, you're a young lad who wants to play football. Suddenly all these cameras, microphones

and notebooks get put in your face, you say something daft or boring and you get crucified for it. Some players aren't too clever and do stupid things but half the time they're encouraged to do them by the press. Then everyone condemns them, says it's no way to behave. They're just footballers, not diplomats or members of the royal family and people forget that.

So I was very happy that no one was allowed to talk to me, it suited me fine. The only trouble was, some newspapers thought there must be a story that was being hidden. They thought because I was a young, dark-haired winger playing for Manchester United, I must be the new George Best off the pitch too. I got followed on holiday, and that's not on. In 1993 one newspaper decided to dig into the private life of my family, which upset me. They can write what they like about me as a footballer, because that's there in the open and subject to opinion. But when they start invading my family's privacy and twisting the truth, it's not on at all. We've had reporters over the wall at the back garden of my mum's house. One paper printed a picture of where we lived so people started coming round at all hours. My stepfather's grown pretty good at dealing with those who like to come round at one in the morning. When I see untrue things about my character in the papers I take comfort from the fact that they can't possibly know what I'm like because they've never met me.

In fact the Boss used to be so good at keeping me shielded, at letting me grow at my own pace, that he took a lot of stick. Des Lynam had a go at him every week on Match of the Day. There was even talk that he had created a monster in me, that the very silence was building an image which wasn't true. So now I'm a bit older and more experi-

enced, he has relaxed the restrictions a bit, to let people see what I'm really like. I've done one or two things, interviews with the press and television and I've found you get better at them. You learn from your mistakes, just as you do at football. The Boss even got someone in to give us all lessons in how to talk to television or radio. They did mock interviews with us, then played them back, so they could tell us what we did wrong, telling us how to look into a camera, explaining to us what tricks journalists might use to trip you up.

I was really glad I appeared on *Question of Sport*. The producer had been asking for me since I made my debut in the first team, and the Boss always said no. But this year he thought I was ready and I loved it, though my mum said she was more nervous for me then than when I trotted out at Wembley. My mum, my brother Rhodri and I used to play it at home every week, testing each other. If my mum beat me I'd be furious. It was always my ambition to go on that programme. It takes about an hour and a half to make. They told us beforehand that if we didn't know an answer we shouldn't worry, we should just take our time because they could edit out all the pauses. Well, I couldn't do that, there was an audience there, so if I didn't know anything I just said sorry. But Ian Botham, he spent hours trying to get one particular answer, he was like a dog with a bone, I thought it would be next season by the time he finished. Mind you it proved to me that they don't get fed the answers beforehand.

The Boss also allowed me to do some commercial work. The problem with doing too much is that it can soon interfere with your football because the demands on your time can be quite high. The other day Incey rang me and said, 'Hello, is that Prince?' I didn't know what he was on about. I said 'Prince who?' Apparently there'd been a newspaper article with a group of 'advisers' giving me suggestions on how I could maximise my earnings, how I could land £14 million in five years. One of them said I should do a pop record, get to number one and do a massive tour: the 'Prince' of football. I'm not sure what the manager would say about that. They'd obviously never heard me sing. I wasn't on the United single, C'mon You Reds, which got to number one, incidentally. Eric, Incey and me had to do something else on the day of the recording, and when we heard the result we were rather glad we did.

People who talk about all the money to be made as a celebrity (whatever that is) have no idea. They think you wake up and play football. They think you turn up on a Saturday and that's it. This bloke in the paper said that I could do the pop album in the closed season. He didn't realise that if you've done your job as a footballer at all properly, you're absolutely knackered at the end of the season. The holiday should be just that. The last thing you want to do is go on a pop concert tour.

I've done some work promoting Reebok sports goods, doing photo-shoots for brochures, appearing in their television commercials and so on. The telly advert they did was amazing. I spent all day at Selhurst Park, just having a

kickaround with some Wimbledon youth team players. Then when I saw it on the telly, there I was playing with Law, Best, Charlton, Stevie Coppell and Charlie Mitten. They told me what they intended to do at the time, but I couldn't see it, how they could transform a kickaround into that. I also do six public appearances a year for Reebok, when I turn up at a shop and sign some autographs. It's always fun to meet fans, though it can get out of hand. Actually, it can get a bit mad. At Swansea I went to a sports shop in the city centre and there were about fifteen thousand fans there; people were getting hurt in the crush. I honestly couldn't believe it.

People have started to ask me if I'm not getting a bit over-exposed, with my picture on magazines and posters. It's true sometimes it can be a bit embarrassing having to walk past pictures of yourself. My mum says she's sick of the sight of me, everywhere she goes. But I can't be a real celeb, I've not been approached by *Hello* magazine yet. You know: Footballer Ryan Giggs shows us round his delightful new home. I'm glad about that. With the curse of *Hello* the place would probably fall down as soon as they've been round. And I've only just moved in.

the team

It is probably about time I introduced you to my team-mates. Here for the record is the official Ryan Giggs guide to Manchester United players and their nicknames...

Just before the Cup Final Lee Sharpe wrote an article in the paper listing what he claimed were all the players' nick-names. He said that I was called Wasim, after Wasim Akram the Lancashire and Pakistan cricketer. Well, that was the first I'd heard of it. In fact he made up half the nicknames in that article. I think he just thought of a few silly names on the spur of the moment, took the money and legged it.

Anyway, Peter Schmeichel doesn't have one. Call him names and he'd batter you. Peter takes life very seriously and is not often happy. Sometimes in the afternoon a group of us will do some extra training, mostly shooting practice. Peter, who is a brilliant trainer, comes and helps us. The trouble is that Incey and Roy Keane like to wind him up by clattering the ball as hard as possible at him from as short a range as possible. Sometimes, quite often actually, Peter gets fed up with this treatment and takes his gloves off, muttering. I have to say his grasp of English is very good, judging by some of the things he mutters on his way back to the dressing room.

If he's around, we'll drag out Les Sealey. Peter is a superstitious character, if you notice he kicks the bottom of each goal-post every time he goes out on the pitch. But Les is riddled with superstition. In fact he's called Lucky Les and reckons he's the manager's lucky mascot; he's forever reminding us that ever since he arrived at the club in 1989, the Boss hasn't stopped winning things.

At right back is Paul Parker, or, as Incey calls him, Benny, because he is a ringer for a character on the children's telly show Grange Hill. We discovered at a couple of celebration parties recently that Parks is a terrible dancer. Dion Dublin and Incey take the mick out of him something terrible about it. In fact the joke about him is that he is a black man who dances like a white man.

Denis Irwin is called Pogo, another telly lookalike, another Grange Hill character. Mr Reliable, he is, the best left back in Britain. Either Denis, Eric or I take all the direct free kicks at the club. It usually depends where the offence has taken place. If it is to the right of the box, I'll take it; to the left or centre, Denis will; and if Eric says he fancies it, we leave it to him wherever it is. You tend to do that with Eric. But the way I've been taking free kicks recently, and the way he has, I think people would prefer it if I left my share to Denis.

Gary Pallister used to be referred to as Dolly Daydream, because he can appear to drift off into another world. More recently he has become Crazy Legs, like Crazy Legs Crane the cartoon character. This again becomes obvious for anyone who has seen him dance. He thinks he's the business on the dancefloor, but he's got such a long body, and his arms and legs are so all over the place, that even if he had any rhythm he'd look like an octopus dangling on the end of a fishing line. Actually Pally thinks he's a male model all round. All that tall, blond, blue-eyed stuff. But he's got the worst dress sense in the club. He buys loads of smart, expensive gear, anything with a label, and wears it all wrong, matches the wrong shirt with the wrong pants and bottoms it all off with the wrong pair of shoes. Just because

it's Armani, we tell him, doesn't mean it looks good.

Steve Bruce, the long-serving and much-respected captain is known as Big Al, another character off Grange Hill, Tucker's mate. The most superstitious of the lot, is Brucie. We always have to wait for him, because, as captain, he leads us out on to the pitch. This is his routine in the dressing room just before we go out: the bell goes to tell us it's time to go, so he goes to the toilet; he comes back, puts his shirt on, goes to the toilet; he comes back, has a drink, goes to the toilet, comes back, puts his arm out so Norman the kitman can put the captain's arm band on him, goes to the toilet, comes out and then says, 'Oh you're all waiting for me are you lads?'

Roy Keane is Damien, the devil incarnate off the film *The Omen*. He's evil. Even in training, in shooting practice he'll stand a couple of yards from the keeper and smack it as hard as he can. He's mad. But he's funny, too. His latest joke is at Pally's expense. He gets in the bath after training and will whisper, 'Watch this,' to me or Sharpey. Then he will start singing a snippet of a song he may have heard on the car radio on the way in. A couple of minutes later, Pally will be getting changed or towelling himself down and off he goes, singing the song Roy was singing. Absolutely guaranteed to work every time.

Paul Ince is my best mate around the club. We share a room at hotels for away games, and we share a sense of humour all the time. He is my minder on the pitch (actually he's everyone's minder on the pitch) and in training if I have a little tussle with someone, I'll sing, 'Incey, Incey sort him out,' like the fans do. We play golf together but he cheats by being better than me. He has a golf course near his house and practises sneakily there before we play. I've only taken up the game recently and quite enjoy it. But I liked George Best's line on it. Someone asked him if he played and he said no, he couldn't see the point, he hated having to part with the ball. Incey has his superstitions, too. He always insists on going out on to the pitch last, putting on his shirt in the tunnel. I don't know what would happen if we signed someone else who liked to go out last, the two of them would be stuck in the tunnel all match saying, 'After you'. He's the one who makes up all the nicknames. With typical modesty, he calls himself the Guvnor. But since we saw a picture of him as a baby in the *Manchester United* magazine, we've been calling him Jacko because he looked the spit of Michael Jackson when he was a little kid. He doesn't look anything like Michael Jackson now. But then Michael Jackson doesn't look anything like Michael Jackson now either.

Andrei Kanchelskis speaks more English than he lets on and he's really settled in at the club now. We're all rather

jealous of him because he has the best chant from the fans. They sing his name to this Russian tune and then shout 'Hoi' like a bunch of crazed Cossacks on the steppes. When he scores one of his screamers in training we all sing that. In fact the fans really got behind him when there was a chance he might leave at the end of last season, and I think that helped him decide to stay. We're all just relieved he did. He's got a rocket shot on him, and could probably score a free kick from the halfway line.

Mark Hughes has been called Sparky, because he's so electric, for years. Recently he has become known as The Ledge, as in legend. And rightly so. He's awesome. He was

my hero when I was young. I used to worship him from the Stretford End and it hasn't changed much since.

My other United hero when I was a kid was Bryan Robson, and as with Hughes, when I got to know him and play with him, nothing changed my opinion. He has gone now to manage Middlesbrough, and he will be badly missed around the place at Old Trafford. We had a great party after the Cup Final, but for me it was a bit sad as well because it was the last time Bryan Robson was around. He gave a speech thanking everyone, which was well moving. Robson was a big father figure around Old Trafford, every-one looked up to him. When I first went into the first team,

if I had any questions, I went straight to him and he was always willing to help. He advised me on all sorts of aspects of my career, not just the playing side. He was the first person I'd go to, and I'm not the only one. I know he helped Incey a lot when he first arrived at the club. Management material all right.

Another player who's gone now but will be missed is Mickey Phelan. What people don't realise about Mickey is he's a class dresser. Everyone who sees him on the pitch thinks because of his hair, or lack of it, he'll dress like a middle-aged man. Wrong: Mickey wears top gear.

Lee Sharpe: well, I can't think of a nickname for him. Anyone who's seen him off the pitch will know a cricketer's name wouldn't be appropriate, he's a bit too fast to be a cricketer. Let's just call him mad and leave it at that.

Then we come to Eric Cantona. He's known by Brucie and some of the others simply as Ooh-Aah, after his chant. Everything about Eric is cool. Unlike, say, Pally, he can wear anything and look the business. He came into training the other day in ripped jeans, a denim shirt, a denim jacket and trainers and looked a different class. If anyone else had worn that they wouldn't have got away with it. To play with him is a dream. Eric is the extra dimension in our team. When he was out suspended toward the end of last season, you could see that. And when he came back it lifted us all.

He is the best passer I have ever seen. He brings people into the game, up front, midfield, wherever he goes, he gives us so much variety. People try to put a block on him, but he's forever thinking of ways to evade his marker, create space for himself. And while they're concentrating on him, they forget about Sparky or Andrei who revel in the extra space, so they might be better off leaving him to it. When Eric gets the ball he is brilliant at putting it out on to the wing. He can judge how fast we can run - me, Sharpey, Andrei - and he puts balls out to us so perfectly weighted it means we don't even have to break stride. I think he knows how fast the full back can run too.

Often when Eric gets the ball you can't conceive that a pass is on, but you have to make the run, get ahead of the defender because just as he looks as if he's lost it, he'll pop it through his marker's legs and out to you. And if you're not ready for it, he'll roast you.

He's such a strong personality, Eric. When we won the title the first time, it was just after he'd arrived and a lot of us players, including me, were saying: 'OK, but when the going gets tough, where will he be?' It's proved exactly the opposite. Given the amount of stick he got in the press, he had to be a big man to shrug that off. And I've never known a player want to get involved like he does, demanding the ball all the time. Even if he's having a bad game, he'll work hard for the team. He didn't even have that good a game in the Cup Final against Chelsea, but when it came to taking the penalties, he grabbed the ball. There was no question in his mind he was going to take them, and no doubt in my mind he was going to score. Brucie couldn't watch. He sat on the halfway line, facing the other way. But I could watch. With Eric, you know it will go in.

All that stuff about 'the ball responding to my touch like a woman to the caresses of a man she loves', makes us laugh too but the thing about Eric is he works so hard to justify the poetry. When you see Eric Cantona staying on for extra training, brushing up on his skills, it makes you realise you can't be satisfied with what you're doing.

In the end, though, it doesn't matter what we call each other, who can dance or who dresses well. For a football team what counts is what we do on the pitch. And there I think the main strength, the one that sets us apart, is that there are so many good individuals but we still play well as a side. Even if two or three of us aren't playing well, there's always someone who can score a spectacular goal or create something out of nothing.

As I said, it's a dream to be part of this team.

the double

It was definitely less tense this season, whatever the media may have said. It was a very different season from the first year we won the title, too. Then we were bottom of the league after the first three games; Norwich were top for a while; finally it was a fight between us and Villa. This year, we were ahead from start to finish, and it only became a dog fight towards the end...

Somehow there's a very different sense of what you need to do when you're ahead than when you're chasing. What's more I think we were a better team this year, more accomplished, better at pressing home advantages, better at making sure a lead counted.

We still made mistakes, though. It was horrible to lose against Galatasaray, a terrible cock-up. They went into the European Cup mini-league and only scored one goal in six matches, which showed they weren't up to much. Really we blew it at Old Trafford, we were 2-0 up and their geezer

scored from 35 yards. If that hadn't gone in we'd have won it because they weren't going to score at their place if it had gone on all month.

The night before the game in Istanbul we got death threats at the hotel. When the phone rang in the room, I just handed it to Incey and he gave whoever was calling an earful. Luckily my mum didn't ring. A lot of the press said that we were intimidated in the game there by the atmosphere. But it didn't worry me, as I've said, the louder it is, the more I prefer it. In fact it was brilliant there. Well, brilliant for them.

The chants went all round the ground, everyone singing together like a choir, with all these drums going all the time.

They were a fanatical bunch all right, the Turks. On the ride back to the airport, they threw all sorts of things at the coach. And I don't mean sticks of celery. Brucie had his head against the window and someone threw a rock at him, cracked the window. Imagine taking time to throw things at the coach when you've won. God knows what would have happened if we had turned them over. In domestic competition though, things went well. But we had to be careful.

The press had built us up so much - by Christmas we'd won it, we were the greatest, best team ever - that there had to be a backlash. And it came. Eric got sent off twice, we lost the Coca Cola Cup, Andrei got sent off, we lost to Blackburn and suddenly we were a bunch of moaners who didn't deserve to win anything, let alone the treble. Everyone was coming out of the woodwork to have a go.

It's hard, but you have to try and ignore it. It's easier to close your mind to it when it's bad press than good. But you have to be just as careful about the good press, because if

you start to believe it you can become complacent. If we had believed what we read at Christmas, that the championship was as good as ours, then Blackburn would be Champions now.

From March onwards, however, we didn't have to worry about good press. It became like a state of siege, everyone hated us. And funnily enough, I think it motivated us, because I honestly don't think all the complaints about us being moaners were justified. The thing about football at the level we're playing it is that every single game is vital. So every single decision within that game is vital. And when it goes against you, you're fired up, desperate to win and you tend to express your disappointment. It's not that we moan, it's the emotions of the moment. After the game, when you see the replay and you see the ref is right, you think: 'Oh, I shouldn't have done that'. But when you're in the game or coming off the pitch, you're in the thick of it. You can't be impartial out there, when every game you play is crucial. It's true the pressure we're under is nothing compared to the lads at the bottom of the league, but one thing I know for sure is we wouldn't be at the top if we were all

laid back and let it flow all over us.

I think we're a fair team. We don't waste time, we don't play act, we don't dive for penalties (well, except Andrei, once) which other teams do. We were only given four penalties all season, and two of those were in the Cup Final, which shows we don't go hunting for them. During all the attacks on us, I heard Phil Thompson say the most sensible thing. He said Liverpool used to moan all the time in their heyday. It comes with success. You want more of it, your whole outlook is geared towards achieving more. You live a bit on edge.

But we knew that the best answer to the critics was on the pitch. And the moment that turned things right again for us after that dodgy spell was the goal in the FA Cup semi by Mark Hughes. That's exactly what I meant about our team: several of us can be having a horrible game, but someone will do something brilliant to save us. I thought we'd blown it then, but Sparky's goal changed everything. For a start, a replay gave us breathing space in the Premiership. We were due to play Leeds on the Wednesday and to go there after playing Wembley, which

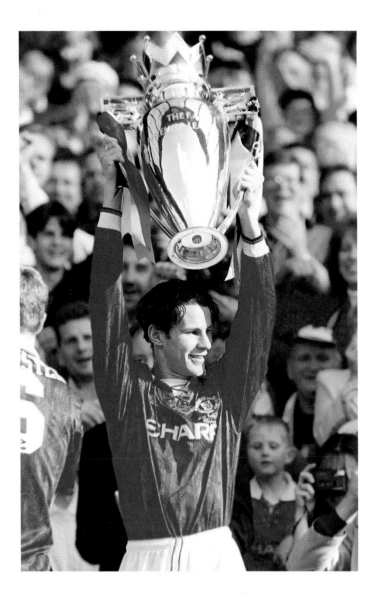

exhausts you. It would have been very difficult. Instead we played Oldham, who were just as knackered as we were, and it gave us a chance to rest before playing Leeds. Also it meant that Eric was available for an extra league game after his suspension. To go to Leeds without Eric was not an appealing prospect.

From the replay on we just seemed to get stronger and stronger. Which is what happened in 1993. A lot of the media were predicting we'd crack and some of the players

couldn't work out what they were on about: we'd done it last year, we were by far the best team, why should we crack? We should have wrapped things up earlier than we did by winning against Wimbledon. But I thought it was on the cards we'd lose there. As we found out that day in 1992 when we lost at Liverpool, it's really no fun going out for a vital match knowing what your rivals have done a couple of hours earlier. We went out against Wimbledon knowing Blackburn had lost at Southampton and that if we won

it that was more or less it. But it was a horrible pitch, horrible game, they stopped us from playing, it was frustrating all round and they won it.

Then Eric came back from suspension, scored against City, and against Leeds we were fantastic, giving perhaps our best performance of the season. They put Fairclough on Eric, but even though he didn't get that much room for himself, they were so worried about him, they gave room to Sparky and me and Andrei. That's another brilliant thing

about this United side, no one really knows what to do against us. Shut down one person and another will do the business.

Against Ipswich, I got my goal of the season. It may seem strange to say that about a toe-poke from five yards, but I was pretty chuffed with that goal. It meant a lot to win the game. We went 1-0 down, then Eric got it back to 1-1. And every time they attacked, we were getting nervous. I was on the touch-line where the Boss was, he was giving me some

stick, I wasn't having that good a game. So when the ball came over and I got my leg in front of the defender and put it away, I was well chuffed. What pleased me most was that I was getting into goal-scoring positions, the Lineker and Rush places where you can do damage. And then the Boss brought me off.

Blackburn then faced real pressure, perhaps for the first time in the season. They knew they had to win against Coventry on the Monday night to stay in it. Up until then, it hadn't really mattered for them. If they kept winning, that was brilliant; they were keeping the race open. If they lost, well they weren't expected to be able to plug such a huge gap. Suddenly it had come to a head and they had to win. The sort of pressure Blackburn were under that night, you've got to have experienced it to appreciate it. And they'll be stronger for it. Again that night I went to my mate's house. But this year I was sufficiently relaxed to watch the whole game. Blackburn lost it, and for the second year running we won the Championship without playing. For the second year running, we all ended up at Brucie's place.

So I picked up my second successive Premiership award. Last year it was a little miniature of the trophy. I liked it, but some of the lads complained, saying it wasn't traditional enough. So this year they gave us gold medals with a lion on them. Very nice. I now had two Championship medals, a League Cup winners' medal and a Youth Cup winners' medal. I was very keen to complete the set.

I went out to the Cup Final really fired up. I was desperate to prove to myself that I could play at Wembley. I'd been substituted in the Coca Cola Cup Final, and the Charity Shield, and I'd only really come into the FA Semi there in extra time. The manager had a quiet word before the game, he just said, 'Come on, let's get this Wembley jinx of yours out of the way. Play well, play your normal game.'

Those are the motivations, they come from inside you, your own standards and ambitions. It was brilliant that day. We won the Cup, we won the double, we were in the history books. And what's more, I wasn't substituted.

From my own point of view, I had a bit of an up-and-down season. I scored more goals than ever, was there when we won the big games. But in the middle of the campaign, I felt very tired. I started getting dizzy spells, and got a lot of headaches, a lot of sore throats. It was diagnosed as my tonsils playing up. At the end of the season I had them removed. They were so infected that, after they took them out, the hospital sent them away for tests. To Sellafield, I think.

fans

It's not just opposing players who try to put you off your stride, it's the opposing fans too. They get up to some well dodgy things these days. And because I take the corners, I seem to come into contact with them more than most...

At the Cup Final, for instance, I went over to take a kick where the Chelsea fans were and they started chucking things at me. Nothing unusual there, except these missiles

weren't the usual plastic cups and cans, they were sticks of celery and sweetcorn. I don't know what that was about, but it made me laugh to think of them popping into green-grocer's shops on the way to Wembley. At Anfield things tend to be a bit more basic. They throw 50ps at me there, yelling abuse. I have my own way of dealing with that: I put the ball down, take one step, kick it and then run off to the safety of the penalty area where I've only got Neil Ruddock to worry about.

Generally, though, I've found that crowds have been much less hostile towards us this year. Sometimes I even hear encouragement coming from opposing fans.

Having said that, someone took a swing at Sparky at Swindon, which isn't on, and the reaction to Incey at West Ham was well out of order. It was his first game back there since his transfer four years ago and they gave him a hor-rible return with all that racist nonsense, which I thought had gone out of the game. It didn't put him off his stride though, he's such a strong character. He answered them back in the best possible way, scoring in the last minute. When we lost the championship at West Ham a couple of years ago, by the end of the game there was a bank-load of coins thrown on the pitch. Next time we play there we'll have to get Norman the kitman to stitch pockets in our shorts, like rugby players have, then we won't be short for a round after the game.

West Ham are perhaps the most hostile crowd we face apart from Leeds. They do hate us at Leeds. In their Kop End there's about 15,000 skinheads just yelling abuse at you when you go to take a corner. Mind you I'd much rather have that than going somewhere where there's no atmosphere. There's nothing worse than that. At Anfield, Elland Road, Upton Park and Maine Road the atmosphere

really gets the adrenalin pumping, it makes you feel that there's something important at stake, as though what you're doing matters. In fact I think I like playing at Elland Road best of all away grounds. I've always done well there. It is partly because we always seem to play there at night, and I prefer playing at night. I feel more relaxed. You have a lie-in in the morning of the game, have something to eat,

then go back to bed. So you feel much fresher for night games. Plus we tend to win there. And since they hate us so much at Leeds, it feels all the better putting one over on them.

Nowhere I've played, though, even the Cup Final, matched the atmosphere when we played in South Africa just before last season. Everything about that trip was amazing, apart from the flight. United had never been there because of the sporting boycott over apartheid and no one had a clue how popular football, or Manchester United, were. It was unbelievable. It's mainly the blacks who follow football, the whites prefer rugby, and everywhere we went they just went mad. They were fanatical. When we played Kaiser Chiefs the crowd was amazing. There was a witch

doctor in all the traditional gear and he stood at the bottom of the stand and conducted the crowd through these brilliant chants. He was astonishing. And the stadium was massive, right in the middle of Soweto, and after all you've heard about Soweto, somehow the last thing you expected was this huge modern football stadium. I met Nelson Mandela there, and when we were introduced he said he had heard of me. That was nice, because I'd heard of him. He was a lot taller than I'd imagined, about six foot one. He'd have made a brilliant target man in his day. And considering he's in his seventies and was in prison most of his life, he's in brilliant shape. He said that after Kaiser Chiefs, his team, he supported United. So there you have it. The most famous man in the world follows United.

If the crowd get going, I love it. Noisy games are best for me. Our supporters when we're playing away from home are fantastic, usually out-sing the home supporters, make loads of noise and really get behind the team. When you hear them chanting your name it gives you some lift. I first heard the chant they have for me - Ryan Giggs Running Down The Wing sung to the old Robin Hood theme - in the middle of the 1993 season and it took me ages to work out what they were singing. I know it doesn't rhyme, but when I hear that it makes me think I'm doing something worthwhile.

At Old Trafford it tends to be a bit more of a family atmosphere. Before we won the title, there was a tendency for fans to get on top of the players if things went wrong. Back

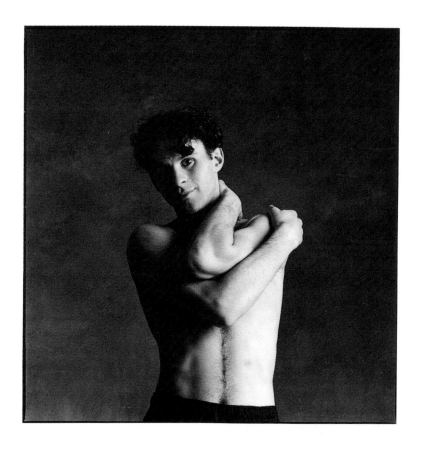

then it could get very tense and quiet at home: you needed to win a game, and if you missed a chance you could hear the groaning. It definitely gets to you, makes you even more tense. To an extent I can understand it, though, the fans in the stand probably suffer more than we players do because they can't do anything about what's going on down on the pitch. I can get the ball and try to effect the result. They just sit on their seats chewing their nails. I feel for them. I know I hate watching, I'm a terrible spectator. It's far worse watching than playing. On the subs' bench you

can't do anything. Or if you're injured, it's horrible.

Last season I sensed Old Trafford was a more relaxed place with the 26-year thing gone. It can still be quiet, but several times last year I thought the roof was going to come off. When we played Everton after Sir Matt Busby died the atmosphere was amazing. The minute's silence was incredibly emotional; every single person inside the ground was completely quiet. The Everton fans deserve a lot of respect for that. It wasn't their day, but they behaved brilliantly, which I suppose shows the degree to which Sir Matt was loved by everyone, not just United fans. Then when the game started, the cheering and chanting was deafening.

The best atmosphere at Old Trafford last season, though, was against Charlton, in the FA Cup Quarter Final. When Peter Schmeichel was sent off, the crowd really got behind us. He got his marching orders just before half-time, and it seemed to spark the fans. As we went in to the dressing room at half-time you could see them really encouraging us. You could see on their faces how much Manchester United meant to them and how important it was for them that we win. In the dressing room the Boss didn't need to say anything to gee us up, we were all fired up. As soon as we went out we scored and went on to win it. That's when you need help, when you're up against it. And I think there's no question the fans got us through that one.

So, if you're one of Old Trafford's singers and chanters: maximum respect. We couldn't do it without you.

love

This is going to be short and sweet...

On Valentine's day I got about 6,000 cards, which was incredibly flattering. Some of them were very funny, some were, well, I'll leave it to your imagination. It's a strange thing to be the object of lots of girls' affections, though to be honest I think much of it is because I'm young and play for Manchester United.

As far as girlfriends are concerned, I can make one amazing revelation: I have them. But that's all I'm prepared to say.

My private life I prefer to keep just that - private. And I am getting a little fed up with press photographers jumping into the cab every time I'm out with a girl, as if this is the most incredible news in the world. I also object to the way any girl who is linked with me gets photographers on her doorstep and her picture plastered all over the papers. I've grown sort of used to it, but they haven't and it's not really on.

Get the message?

the future

Someone asked me if there was anything I wished I had known five years ago. The answer was: well, nothing. There's a football saying about taking each game as it comes and, no matter how many times it has been said before, you have to carry that philosophy with you, because football is a life where it can all go horribly wrong at any time...

You never know what's round the corner. Look at that player from Oldham, Pedersen. He thought he just had a couple more league games to go this season and then he was off to the World Cup with Norway. Then he did his leg in, and it was all over. It happens like that. One fall: bang, dreams gone. One stud in the wrong place: smash, plans out of the window. So you don't plan, then everything comes as a surprise.

While things are going your way, I believe you should enjoy them. Being a footballer is the best possible life. You get paid very well for doing what you love above all, you get time to yourself, you get to meet a lot of famous and interesting people, and, if you play for Manchester United, you get to play alongside the best in your business. So I enjoy myself. I relax with my mates, I go to the local pub where

everyone knows me and no one treats me differently, I go to the cinema, I go to clubs, I like soul music. I go to concerts, too. The last one I went to was Simply Red. And that's fair enough as Mick Hucknall often comes to see us play. He was fantastic, by the way.

I also have a bit of a weakness for clothes. I only dress up about twice a week. Most of the time, after training and so on, I prefer t-shirts, sweats and trainers, sports wear. But when I do dress up, I go for it. Like Eric, who modelled for Paco Rabanne, I wouldn't mind getting up on the catwalk one of these days. If anyone would have me.

I get fashion ideas from magazines like GQ, Arena, Esquire. I've made some bad buys, I have to confess. I bought myself this shirt, for example. It's lime green. It looked great in the shop, it looks good on other people, but it just doesn't suit me. My best shirt is a black one with a grandad collar I bought after an away game in London. Clothes are my main indulgence. When I was living with my mum, I didn't spend that much. It's a bit more expensive now I'm on my own. There's the takeaways for a start.

If I wasn't a footballer I don't know what I'd be. I can't see what else I would have done. For as long as I can remember, I was set on being a footballer. What's more, there was nothing else I was any good at. I played rugby when I was younger, but it's not a full time job and anyway, I don't think I could have made it as a rugby player because I'm not that big in the upper body and those guys are massive. If I played rugby I think I'd have to sit out on the wing and whenever someone came in to crunch me, I'd step out into touch, like they do in American football. I wouldn't mind being a golfer; it looks like a good life from the outside. The trouble is when I play with my mates they usually beat me; when I play with Incey he usually beats me. So if I can't beat that lot, I don't think I would stand much chance earning my living against the likes of Olazabal, Woosnam and Faldo. So I think I'll stick to football.

Because at twenty, I've already got my hands on all the domestic honours, people often ask me whether I have any football ambitions left. Well, I've got loads. First off I want to win the European Cup with United. Fortunately, after blowing it this year, we have another chance to do ourselves justice immediately. I want to qualify for a major interna-

tional championship with Wales and in the process I want to score more than 25 goals for United. I'm desperate to be top scorer at Old Trafford. Looking back on last season, I could easily have scored 25 goals if I'd been more like Lineker or Rush, more clinical. I missed a lot of chances now I think about it. I missed a sitter against Liverpool, a header against Norwich and the worst ever was against Wimbledon in the Cup, a shameful display. I've hit the post twice and the crossbar twice. I know no one ever scores with every chance, but the great players have a high proportion of hits. To increase my scoring rate will take work, more work and a bit of luck.

One ambition I haven't got concerns Italian football. I'm always being asked about Italy and when I'm off there, but to be honest it never enters my mind that I might go. The reason I don't think about it now is I've got no intention of going anywhere for the next few years, so what's the point thinking about it? With football you don't know what's going to happen, you really don't. People say: 'But what about in three or four years' time?' What's the point of even saying 'Maybe'? Three years ago, I wasn't even in the first team. Maybe in three years' time I won't be.

I'm not even sure the football's better over there. I watch a lot of Italian football and there's not a lot of opportunity for wingers, the sweeper system cancels out your space. Technically it's the best league in the world, the best goals are scored there, but it's not necessarily the best place in the world to be a winger who likes living in Manchester. People say the best players in the world play there. But I certainly don't feel any need inside me to prove myself there. After all, if Eric Cantona, Mark Hughes, Paul Ince and Andrei Kanchelskis play for Manchester United, it's good enough for me.

One more thing: I don't think I've finished learning my trade. I know I've got a lot to learn. The manager is always

pointing out to me things that I should or should not be doing. The most important qualities in a professional footballer are determination and dedication. I had to work really hard with my football and I still do. Of course, skill is something you are born with, but you have to practise and practise if you really want to make the most of it. You have

to listen to your coaches and not assume you know everything about the game. Because you don't. And there's no gain without pain.

But pain is soon forgotten when you win. Success is a very addictive thing. You become more and more desperate for it, especially at Manchester United and especially

with the Boss driving you on. If we players start to get complacent, or relax, he's straight in there. He says things like: 'If you don't want it, there's five other players who could easily come in for you.' At United you can feel it behind you. You know they are there, real quality players who could come in quite easily who do want it. That's what makes us a good side: there's this internal pressure. If I'm not doing well, Sharpey can come in; if Sparky isn't Dion can; if Roy has a bad patch there's Brian McClair. You've got to want. You can feel that queue behind you. There's some brilliant kids here and as the Boss demonstrated with me, his motto is: if you're good enough, you're old enough. If you have a bad game, you start to worry and have sleepless nights. In some teams players know whatever they do they'll be in the next week; however much they hide, they'll be around another time. They can go through the motions. You can't do that at United.

And I tell you, once you've tasted being successful for Manchester United, you don't let that go easily. You keep at it, to make sure you're part of it. Next year and for as long as possible.

birthdate: 29 November 1973

birthplace: Cardiff

height: 5'11"

weight: 10st 6lbs.

Captain of the England Under 15 Schoolboy side. In his nine matches in charge, the team won seven including victories against Germany, Holland, France and Belgium.

Manchester United record

debut: as sub on 2 March 1991 at home to Everton in a 2-0 victory. First full appearance home to Manchester City 4 May 1991, scoring the only goal of the game.

appearances including as substitute

1990/91:	League 2, 1 goal
1991/92:	League 38, 4 goals; League Cup 8, 3 goals; FA Cup 3; European Cup Winners' Cup 1
1992/93:	League 41, 9 goals; League Cup 2; FA Cup 2, 2 goals; UEFA Cup 1
1993/94:	League 38, 13 goals; League Cup 8, 3 goals; FA Cup 7, 1 goal; European Cup 4
Totals:	League 119, 27 goals
	FA Cup 12, 3 goals
	League Cup 18, 6 goals
	European Cup 4
	European Cup Winners' Cup 1
	UEFA Cup 1

Grand Total: 155 appearances, 36 goals

International record

under 21: one appearance, 30 May 1991, away to Poland. Won 2-1.

first cap: Youngest player to appear for Wales when came on as sub in a European championship qualifier against Germany in Nuremberg 16 October 1991 at 17 years, 332 days old.

first full appearance: Home to Belgium in World Cup qualifier on 31 March 1993. Scored in a 2-0 win.

honours

FA Premier League winner 1992/93

FA Carling Premiership winner 1993/94

FA Cup winner 1994

Rumbelows League Cup winner 1991/92

FA Youth Cup winner 1992

PFA Young Player of the Year 1992, 1993

Barclays Young Eagle of the Year 1993

Bravo Best Young Player in Europe 1993

file

ryan giggs **my bum**